6.0

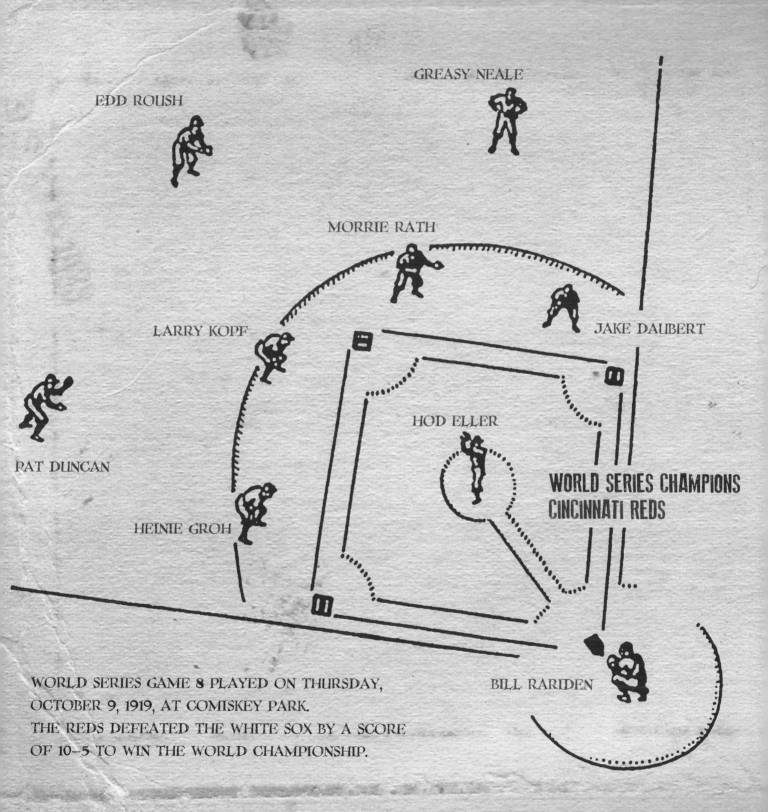

EDD ROUSH

GREASY NEALE

MORRIE RATH

LARRY KOPF

JAKE DAUBERT

PAT DUNCAN

HOD ELLER

WORLD SERIES CHAMPIONS
CINCINNATI REDS

HEINIE GROH

BILL RARIDEN

WORLD SERIES GAME 8 PLAYED ON THURSDAY,
OCTOBER 9, 1919, AT COMISKEY PARK.
THE REDS DEFEATED THE WHITE SOX BY A SCORE
OF 10–5 TO WIN THE WORLD CHAMPIONSHIP.

WORLD SERIES CHAMPIONS

CINCINNATI REDS

SARA GILBERT

CREATIVE EDUCATION

Published by Creative Education
P.O. Box 227, Mankato, Minnesota 56002
Creative Education is an imprint of The Creative Company
www.thecreativecompany.us

Design and production by Blue Design (www.bluedes.com)
Art direction by Rita Marshall
Printed in the United States of America

Photographs by Corbis (Bettmann, Underwood & Underwood),
Getty Images (APA, Chicago History Museum, Diamond Images,
Focus on Sport, John Grieshop/MLB Photos, Heinz Kluetmeier/
Sports Illustrated, Bob Levey, Andy Lyons, MLB Photos, Ronald
C. Modra/Sports Imagery, National Baseball Hall of Fame/MLB
Photos, Lucy Nicholson/AFP, Photo File/MLB Photos, Donavan
Reese, Robert Riger, Joe Robbins, Mark Rucker/Transcendental
Graphics, Joe Robbins, Paul Schutzer/Time & Life Pictures, Tony
Tomsic/MLB Photos, Kevin Winter)

Library of Congress Cataloging-in-Publication Data
Gilbert, Sara.
Cincinnati Reds / Sara Gilbert.
p. cm. — (World series champions)
Includes bibliographical references and index.
Summary: A simple introduction to the Cincinnati Reds major
league baseball team, including its start in 1869, its World Series
triumphs, and its stars throughout the years.
ISBN 978-1-60818-263-3
1. Cincinnati Reds (Baseball team)—History—Juvenile literature.
I. Title.
GV875.C65G55 2013
796.357'640977178—dc23   2011051190

First edition
9 8 7 6 5 4 3 2 1

Cover: First baseman Joey Votto
Page 2: Manager Sparky Anderson
Page 3: Left fielder Adam Dunn
Right: Center fielder Vada Pinson

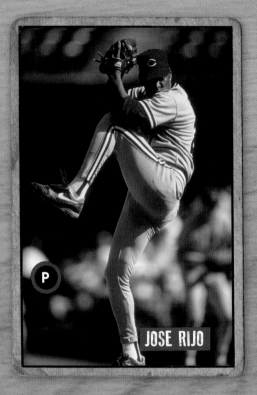

P

JOSE RIJO

1B

TED KLUSZEWSKI

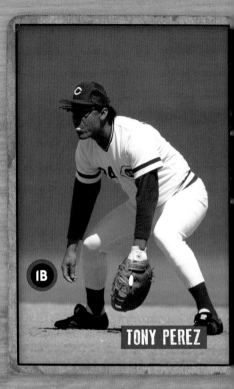

1B

TONY PEREZ

M

BILL McKECHNIE

LF

ADAM DUNN

CF

EDD ROUSH

TABLE OF CONTENTS

CINCINNATI AND GREAT AMERICAN BALL PARK

Cincinnati is a city in Ohio. It was started along the Ohio River in 1788. In 2003, a stadium called Great American Ball Park was built next to the river. A baseball team called the Reds plays there.

RIVALS AND COLORS

The Reds are a team in Major League Baseball. They play against other major-league teams to win the World Series and become world champions. The Reds wear red and white uniforms. Cincinnati fans cheer loudest for games against their RIVALS, the Pittsburgh Pirates.

PITCHERS ROB DIBBLE   NORM CHARLTON

SHORTSTOP BARRY LARKIN

REDS HISTORY

The Reds are the oldest Major League Baseball team. They played their first season in 1869. They won all 57 games that year! They won their first World Series in 1919.

9 AT BAT — 2 STRIKES 3 BALLS 2 OUTS

TEAMS. 1 2 3 4 5 6 7 8 9 10   P. C.   UMPIRES

CINTI 0 0 0 3 0   11 9   PLATE   BASES

CHIGO 0 0 0 0 0 0   14 8   R. LINE 9 L. LINE 7

THIS SCORE BOARD MADE BY M. SCHWAB

E A HIT
WITH—

Puritan
CINCINNATI

EPPA RIXEY

GEORGE FOSTER

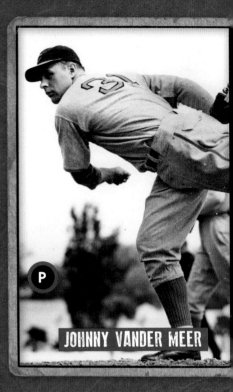

JOHNNY VANDER MEER

DUSTY BAKER

EDWIN ENCARNACIÓN

EDINSON VOLQUEZ

PETE ROSE

The Reds won the championship again in 1940. Star
first baseman Pete Rose led the Reds to World Series
championships in 1975 and 1976. Fans called the team
the "Big Red Machine."

KEN GRIFFEY JR.

The Reds were not as good for the next 15 years. But in 1990, new manager Lou Piniella helped them reach the World Series. The Reds beat the powerful Oakland A's in a big UPSET. Slugging outfielder Ken Griffey Jr. hit his 500th CAREER home run in Cincinnati in 2004. In 2010, the Reds got back to the PLAYOFFS. But they have not been in the World Series since 1990.

FIRST BASEMAN TONY PEREZ

FRANK ROBINSON

ERNIE LOMBARDI

REDS STARS

Strong catcher Ernie Lombardi played in Cincinnati from 1932 until 1941. He won the Most Valuable Player (MVP) award in 1938. Hard-hitting outfielder Frank Robinson was the best ROOKIE in baseball in 1956.

Johnny Bench played all 17 years of his career in Cincinnati. He was one of the best **DEFENSIVE** catchers ever. He played with second baseman Joe Morgan. Morgan was very fast. He was a great batter, too.

First baseman Joey Votto joined the Reds in 2008. In 2010, he hit 37 home runs for Cincinnati and won the MVP award. Fans hoped he would help the Reds return to the World Series soon!

JOE MORGAN

JOHNNY BENCH

JOEY VOTTO

HOW THE REDS GOT THEIR NAME

The Reds were called the Cincinnati Red Stockings at first. They wore white uniforms with tall red socks. In 1890, their name was shortened to the Reds. One of the reasons for the change was that other teams in other cities were also called the Red Stockings.

ABOUT THE REDS

First season: 1869

League/division: National League, Central Division

World Series championships:

1919	5 games to 3 versus Chicago White Sox
1940	4 games to 3 versus Detroit Tigers
1975	4 games to 3 versus Boston Red Sox
1976	4 games to 0 versus New York Yankees
1990	4 games to 0 versus Oakland A's

Reds Web site for kids:

http://mlb.mlb.com/mlb/kids/index.jsp?c_id=cin

Club MLB:

http://web.clubmlb.com/index.html

GLOSSARY

CAREER — all the years a person spends doing a certain job

DEFENSIVE — playing in the field and trying not to let the other team score runs

PLAYOFFS — all the games (including the World Series) after the regular season that are played to decide who the champion will be

RIVALS — teams that play extra hard against each other

ROOKIE — an athlete playing his or her first year

UPSET — a game in which the team that most people think will win ends up losing

INDEX